Contents

D0523979

50p

About Swimming without Stress

When I started studying for my degree in London in 1988, I saw swimming as a way to keep fit and a possible antidote to arduous study of the Thai language. But when I came across an inspiring book by Harvey S Weiner called *Total Swimming* (Simon and Schuster 1981) it opened up a new world to me. This wasn't a book about how to swim better or faster. Weiner encourages all swimmers to think about the quality of experience in water, to enjoy the sensation of the water all around you, massaging and supporting you. The message is that swimming is for everyone and that it is more than just a sport: it can change your life. Guided by the enthusiastic writings of Harvey Weiner, I became addicted to swimming and discovered that moving through the water with my face submerged did something profound for me. My wife Cheryl would frequently join me in our local pool and we have enjoyed swimming together ever since.

In 1991, we went to live in Tokyo with my brother Mike and his wife Chie. By this time, I was training hard for triathlons. I wanted to swim competitively and triathlons were the most appealing way for me to do it. But competitive training goals soon took over and I became obsessed with times instead of enjoying the experience of swimming. While I didn't feel I could go to the pool without a stopwatch and a training plan, Cheryl's approach to swimming remained balanced. My brother, a Zen Buddhist, once pointed out that in my swimming I was "getting the means mixed up with the end". My sister-in-law Chie, a PE teacher and ex- competitive long distance swimmer, sometimes swam with me at our local pool. She seemed to express an attitude towards moving through the water which I had forgotten. She swam beautifully, cutting through the water quietly and softly, but she wasn't interested in measuring her times. It was some years before I would rediscover this approach to swimming.

During this period, working as an English teacher, I found that several of my close colleagues were afraid of water and they were the first people I taught to swim. This was when I realised that fear of water is widespread and that I could help people with it.

In 1995 I had been working in local government for three years, which had already begun to take its toll on my health, when my brother returned to England to train as an Alexander Technique teacher. Chie, Cheryl and myself immediately began taking lessons. The Alexander Technique explores the link between what we are thinking and how we function mentally and physically. In Alexander lessons, the principle of *thinking in activity* is demonstrated. We learn how our habitual thinking patterns disturb the natural poise of the head, neck and back. By changing the way we think as we carry out simple everyday activities like sitting and standing, we can access a calmness, poise and ease of movement we didn't know was in us. We can enjoy moments of freedom from anxiety and tension when our breathing opens up, we become lighter and move easily. From these experiences in lessons, we have to do our best to keep the new thinking going so we can be freer in our everyday lives.

Many of us respond to everyday stimuli with a degree of fear, bizarre though this is. When the head, neck and back relationship is distorted by our inappropriate reactions, we manifest a "startle response". We stiffen our neck and pull our head down into our body. This causes us to shorten and narrow our back, which restricts our breathing. While this fear response has a primitive function that we may occasionally need, it has become for most of us a habitual pattern that, though inappropriate, feels normal and right. Over time this constant misuse of ourselves may lead to stress-related conditions, common examples being back problems and depression.

In 1996 Steven Shaw and Armand D'Angour's revolutionary book *The Art of Swimming – a new direction using the Alexander Technique* (Ashgrove) was first published. Steven Shaw was the first person to formulate a method of teaching swimming based on the Alexander Technique. He re-thought all the major swimming strokes according to the principles of the Alexander Technique and developed a hands-on teaching method for guiding and supporting people through new and unfamiliar movements.

Swimming and the Alexander Technique complement each other for two reasons. The first is that most swimmers have an instinctive fear of drowning. Even top competitive swimmers can be seen to exhibit unnecessary tension as they move the head to inhale. For most people, the habitual tension pattern which distorts the head, neck and back relationship is exaggerated when in water.

Cheryl, Ian and Chie Cross.

People make a lot more effort to swim than they need to because of a lack of trust in the water to support them and anxiety about the process of breathing. The Alexander Technique is a great tool for helping people to become aware of unnecessary tension in water. For people with fear, the hands-on teaching approach of the Alexander Technique and Shaw Method is invaluable.

The second reason is that there is a different set of rules in water. It is a new space to explore – an adventure into a different world – and thus a chance to behave in a non-habitual way. If we allow it to, water supports us. When horizontal in water, we are free from the challenge of staying upright against gravity. This provides a wonderful opportunity to experience length in the spine as the head leads it forward, fish like, and to let go of unnecessary tension. When we swim, we remove ourselves from the stimuli of daily life and the constraints of normal society. Because of the repetitive and predictable nature of the movements we make when swimming and the limited number of stimuli we need to respond to, we can really focus on the quality of our movement. So, while our habitual tension patterns may manifest themselves more strongly in water, it is actually easier to change them.

I trained on Steven Shaw's first Diploma in Aqua Development and Health in 1997, the only swimming training course to be based on the principles of the Alexander Technique. Cheryl and Chie followed in subsequent years. Chie and I also completed the three-year full time training to become teachers of the Alexander Technique.

I founded Swimming without Stress in 1996 with Cheryl when we started teaching swimming to individuals. Mike Cross has always been in the background, influencing our philosophy and bringing new insights, in particular about the relationship between phobia and movement. Chie Cross has been teaching with us since 2000. Between us Cheryl, Chie and I have taught hundreds of people individually to overcome fear of water and/ or swim more smoothly and efficiently. We hope to continue doing so for many years to come.

Ian Cross, December 2004

Ian and Cheryl Cross run residential swimming courses for individual adults and children in Cardigan Bay, West Wales.
Chie Cross takes individual lessons in Oxfordshire.

Contact: admin@swimmingwithoutstress.co.uk
Tel: 01239 613789.
See www.swimmingwithoutstress.co.uk

Also see www.artofswimming.com
Steven Shaw's website.

Acknowledgements

I would like to thank Steven Shaw, for teaching me to swim, and to teach swimming, using the principles of the Alexander Technique; Carl Stringer and Allen Cross for their excellent photography; Cheryl Cross for editing, Cynthia Cross for proof-reading and Britta Sendlhofer for designing the articles.

Why Swim?

In the 21st century we are moving away from traditional fitness activities and taking up those offering more holistic health benefits, yoga and pilates in particular. So you may be pleased to learn that swimming, rather than just forming a central part of a physical training programme, can be an "adventure into a different world."(1). If you are willing to take an alternative approach to being in water, you may find it provides you with all the health benefits you are looking for.

"With the right mental approach experiences may be encountered which are normally associated with the practice of yoga, tai chi and meditation. In the latter context, it is interesting to speculate how the art of swimming would be regarded now if, hitherto unfamiliar to Western Culture, it had been introduced from the East only within the last few decades." (2)

Here are ten holistic health benefits.

1. Learning breathing and relaxation

Aquatic breathing can give you a wonderful combination of energy and relaxation. It works by emphasising the out-breath and letting the in-breath take care of itself. Preoccupation with the in-breath is disastrous in water. So swimming can teach you the principle for life that in order to breathe in, all we need do is let enough air out. The focus of your swimming should be to move in a calm and conscious way so that breathing is relaxed and unforced.

2. Letting go

People in the medical profession see swimming as the safest form of exercise because there should be no downward pressure on any of the joints or jarring of the internal organs. Swimming can be a great way to build aerobic fitness without risk of injury. Physiotherapists recommend movement in water as a useful part of the therapeutic process for patients recovering from injury and for women preparing for and recovering from childbirth. But few swimmers truly recognise the benefits of releasing the head into the water, looking down and gently breathing out. Swimming with the aim of engaging with the water, enjoying its support, letting go of tension and lengthening the spine will do much more for your overall physical and mental health than ploughing up and down the pool clocking the mileage.

3. Improving flexibility

You've got to loosen up if you want to move well in water so swimming should improve your flexibility. The range of movement of any joint is greater when supported by water. Good swimmers keep the length of the body and let loose, long limbs extend out of free joints. When working on, for example, backstroke kick, you learn to move your legs from your hips, soften your hamstrings and free your ankles so your feet are like flippers. To achieve this, you need to apply thought to movement and direct the muscles of your legs to lengthen instead of trying to make progress by tightening them. For swimming movements to work, you have no choice but to loosen up in a way that doesn't feel normal so wouldn't otherwise happen. The suppleness swimming gives you may improve your movement and breathing in daily life.

4. Slowing down

Slowing down in water is inevitable. Just standing in water changes your metabolism. Working against the resistance of the water builds muscle and gives you a cardiovascular work-out but it should also relax you at the same time. Getting into the water and moving through it but working with it is a great way to remove yourself from the stressful stimuli of your everyday life. Give yourself up to a power greater than yourself and allow water to slow you down.

5. Losing weight the easy way

If you are unfit and want to lose weight, swimming can help. Swimming may even be a good activity to get into before taking up any land based fitness programme. People new to running, for example, may find it difficult to achieve the level of gentle aerobic exercise needed either to lose weight or gain fitness. To burn fat, you need to exercise for 20 to 30 minutes, elevating your heart rate but staying well within your aerobic limits, a few times a week. If you were planning to take up running for fitness, to start with, you may be unable to run long enough at the right aerobic level for weight loss: it is difficult not to overdo it. This is why GPs like to check your heart if you are over 35 and want to start running. Swimming can be a very easy way to lose weight. E.g. 20 minutes gentle breaststroke (breathing out into the water) – may produce a heart rate of 120 beats per minute while feeling like a stroll in the park. Try keeping your HR this low on a run! A real stroll in the park, on the other hand, won't give you enough of a work-out.

6. Looking better

With a balanced swimming programme, almost every muscle in the body responds. Swimming should tone your muscles without making you muscle bound.

"It's great for your back, the best general all round exercise. You get a nice, even development of the whole body, arms and legs." (3),

Increasing your lung capacity through aquatic breathing improves your appearance. With better elimination of toxins, your complexion will change. Swimmers often appear fresh faced and younger than their years.

7. Learning to let your head lead

Horizontal movement, with your head in the water and eyes down, is a good way to learn the movement principle of the head leading the spine. Gliding is good for your back, as your spine can lengthen as your head leads it forward in a fishlike way. On land, your head should lead your spine upwards, so that your spine lengthens as you move. This idea is easier to grasp in the water.

Swimming can be a relief from the challenge of being upright against gravity. When you are tired at the end of the day, your head will sometimes be twisted down into your shortened neck. Gliding can help you undo this.

8. Overcoming your habits

To learn a new skill in water, you have to go right back to basics and may discover all kinds of things about yourself. For example, why is there such a strong tendency to pull the arms all the way back to the hips in breaststroke instead of sculling and gliding? The process you need to go through to overcome tension patterns and instinctive responses is very useful for the brain and may give you new awareness in your life.

9. Renewing zest for life and inner confidence

"The water looked as bright and clear as ever and, without pausing to think, I plunged straight in…" (On getting out) "I looked at myself for a long while, no more with shame now, with joy. Although not yet robust, I felt myself capable of becoming so- harmonious, sensuous, beautiful." (4)

Leaving the stresses of life behind with your clothes in the changing room, you can enter the present moment as you enjoy the regular rhythmical movements of your limbs and give yourself up to the support of the water. After swimming, in this worry-free state, you will feel mentally and physically cleansed, energised and ready for life.

10. Treating yourself on a hot day

Francis Kilvert, a curate in Wiltshire in 1860, wrote about "the delicious feeling of freedom in stripping in the open air and running down naked to the sea, where the waves were curling white with foam and the red morning sunshine glowing upon the naked limbs of the bathers" (5)

(1) 1960s Olympic swimmer Murray Rose, see footnote 5.

(2) Dr Mike Hobdell, The Art and Science in Swimming, article in Fusion magazine 1997.

(3) Dr Arnold Illman, orthopaedic surgeon at Brunswick General Hospital, US, quoted in Total Swimming, Harvey S Weiner, Simon and Schuster, 1980.

(4) Andre Gide ,The Immoralist, 1902, translated by Dorothy Bussy, 1930, Penguin.

(5) Quoted in Haunts of the Black Masseur, Charles Sprawson, Jonathan Cape, 1992.

Making Friends with the Water

Great Olympic swimmer Aleksandre Popov said, "The water is your friend. Treat it kindly and it will help you move."

In this lesson we will look at the importance of making friends with the water and learning to do nothing. There are three basic things to work on to improve your relationship with water, before working on your strokes:

- breathing
- placement of head
- gliding and landing

Most people have an instinctive fear of water. The natural response to this is to try hard, tense up and struggle from A to B, hoping swimming will get easier. But unnecessary tension impedes co-ordination so we need to go right back to basics. Making friends with the water means being able to stop trying, breathe naturally and let the water support you.

The greatest challenge in learning to swim better is getting rid of instinctive movement patterns that get in our way. These are linked to anxiety about breathing so this is the first thing we need to look at.

Breathing

Don't…

- take a deep breath
- hold your breath
- *blow* bubbles i.e. force the air out

First, work on breathing out into the water with your feet on the floor and shoulders submerged. Before putting your face in, sing *Ah* for a few seconds. How much air did you need to take in before doing this? Now do just the same with your face in the water. There is no need to take a deep breath before breathing out into the water and the fact that you are breathing out against water doesn't mean you need to force air out. But what you do need to remember is that the resistance of the water slows the out-breath down. So if you sing Ah into the water for a few seconds, you are not going to empty your lungs and when you come up, you don't need to gasp for a lungful of air. In fact, if you can hear yourself breathing in, you may be taking in too much air. As you come out of the water, continue singing through the surface, so that you are breathing out a little bit more air into the atmosphere. Stop raising your head when the sound changes, so your bottom lip and chin remain in the water. This smooth transition through the surface is crucial, as the moment when the face breaks the surface is often one of slight panic. Avoid trying to breathe in too quickly and sucking in water, or pulling your head away from the surface and gasping. Pulling the head back and sucking in air go together as parts of the fear reflex. Breathing out a little into the atmosphere and keeping your neck free mean that the in-breath can happen on its own, without effort.

When thinking about breathing, it is important to think about your neck. Fear or apprehension will cause you to stiffen your neck. A stiff neck hinders breathing. Remembering to keep your neck free will help you in all aspects of your swimming.

When fit people tire easily in water, it is usually because they are hyperventilating. If you don't breathe out freely into the water but gasp for air between strokes, you are starving yourself of oxygen by failing to get rid of the stale,

deoxygenated air. In later lessons, we will look at breathing in relation to strokes and explore how wrong, instinctive patterns with the arms hinder free breathing.

To recap, do…

- keep your neck soft
- breathe out gently into the water
- keep breathing out as you come through the surface
- keep your chin in the water for the in breath
- let air come in on its own instead of gasping

Using your head

The second fundamental skill of swimming we all need to go back to is using the buoyancy of the head. Many people swim to stop themselves from sinking, trying to swim *on* the water, not *in* it. If you don't let your head float, you carry the weight of it and compress your spine. Releasing the heavy weight of your head into the water is the main way to release tension throughout your body. Your neck can then be free and your spine can lengthen as you move. Swimming teachers often teach flotation with the goal of horizontality – star shapes, etc. This can lead to a feeling that tension is needed in order to float.

Regaining the feet from the glide.

When swimming, momentum will take care of your legs so it doesn't matter if they sink when you do nothing. But most of us need to remember, or find out, that the head floats, if we allow it to.

The following procedure is a good way to learn about the buoyancy of your head. Lie in shallow water face down, not trying to float but looking at the pool floor and pretending that's where you want to go. In other words, give yourself permission to sink. To experience for the first time the buoyancy of your head, you actually need to wish for it to sink. I often put the palm of my hand 12 inches below the surface and invite pupils to try and touch it with their face, to pretend there is something in it they want.

Children are often frustrated by their buoyancy when attempting to pick up an object from the pool floor. If they look down at the object, the top of their head will be pointing forwards, not down, so they will be unable to reach it. They need to learn how to dive down. (This isn't something that can happen by accident!)

Whenever you are prone in water, remember to relax your neck, give your head to the water and look at the floor. It is useful to have an idea about the part of the anatomy where we 'let the head go' from. The skull connects with the top bone of the neck higher than many of us imagine, up between the ears. If your neck is free, there should be the potential for someone else to come along and move your head around in the water.

Gliding and landing

The glide is your chance to experience movement without effort, enjoy releasing tension and be free from the task of co-ordinating your limbs. It is also a prerequisite for swimming with good style as this always includes a non-doing, gliding phase.

Stand tall but relaxed. Let your arms float in the water in front of you. Holding them tense is like putting the brakes on. Keep them pointing forward but loose. Think of your shoulders staying soft and going away from each other. Avoid pinching your shoulder blades together. Stay tall and keep sending your arms forward as you go silently into the water, breathing gently without taking a deep breath first! Let the crown of your head and your fingers point where you want to go as you look down at the floor. Push into the floor or wall with your feet and keep breathing gently until you lose momentum. Don't kick, as the object is to do nothing. Just let your legs lengthen and, with ankles soft, send your toes away. Allow your back to be long and wide. Think of your pelvis as part of your back.

When landing, avoid the tendency to pull your head out of the water first. Instead, watch your knees come forward together, counterbalance with your arms and raise your head only when your feet are planted on the floor. Think of going down to land, not getting out for air.

When you are able to glide freely and regain your feet calmly, you will have the basics of swimming without stress.

On Your Back

Resting on your back.

To be a balanced and confident swimmer, you need to be able to move well on your back. Swimming some backstroke should give you a nice change from front crawl or breaststroke and allow you to exercise and release different muscles. On your back you can enjoy the support of the water without needing to co-ordinate yourself to take in air.

Unfortunately, many swimmers are not quite able to get the most from being supine in water. It is easy to see how fear creates tension when swimming prone, when you need to get your breathing right. In fact, swimming on the back presents just as many difficulties.

When prone, once your face is in the water and you're breathing out freely, releasing your head further is easy if you remember to do it. On the back, while your head should float with your face just clear of the surface, you need a lot of trust in the water to let your head go until it is actually supported. If you hold yourself just a little bit on the back to ensure that the water doesn't envelop your face, the tension will spread throughout your body, spoiling your flotation, breathing and enjoyment. The problem is intensified when backstroke arms are brought into the equation.

Using The Alexander Technique

Named after its founder, FM Alexander (1869 – 1955), the Alexander Technique is a practical method for developing kinaesthetic awareness, co-ordination, balance and poise. It helps us to eradicate harmful habits and redirect our energy so that we can move better and breathe more easily. An increasing number of sports people use the technique for a different approach to movement and performance. It gives us the ability to think our way out of unhelpful movement patterns.

Using the Alexander Technique, we attempt to stop interfering with the proper relationship between the head, neck and back in movement and during rest. When we go wrong on our backs in the water, the pattern of unwanted tension that frequently occurs in our daily life is magnified. Under stress, we all stiffen our neck, pull our head down into our body, shorten our spine and narrow our shoulders. As a consequence, we tighten our limbs and, most significantly, hold our breath. Alexander talked about "the true and primary movement in each and every act". This involves the neck staying free,

the head leading the spine into length instead of clamping down on it and the back widening so breathing is ongoing and unforced.

Many of us are 'too busy' to think about any of this in our daily lives. So we rush from one task to the next in a perpetual state of unnatural tension. But recreational or fitness swimming can be an opportunity for us to practise changing our approach to life. If we don't, it may do us more harm than good. Consider this view, of Alexander Technique teacher Patrick MacDonald.

"All strenuous exercise will reinforce the existing co-ordination of the body or lack of it. The amount of mal-coordination present and the strenuousness of the exercise will determine the good or harm that will result." (The Alexander Technique As I See It, (Rahula, 1989)

Land work

If we can work for a better head, neck and back relationship on land, we can easily learn to use it in water. Wilfred Barlow in *The Alexander Principle* (Gollancz 1973) acknowledges that in modern life we inevitably become over - tense and emphasises the importance of being able to return to a balanced state of rest. This means becoming aware of unwanted tension throughout the head, neck and back and letting it go. Alexander recommended lying down on a hard surface with feet on the floor, knees up and the head gently raised on a few books.

Think of your neck being free without doing anything to free it. Give the weight of your head to the books. Be aware of the wholeness of your back, including your pelvis. Think the crown of your head away from your spine and allow your back to spread out against the floor, lengthening and widening. Send the shoulders one away from the other. Point your knees up to the ceiling. Any Alexander Technique teacher will be glad to help you with this.

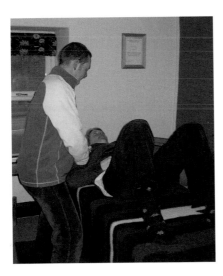

Swimming on your back

Water can help us to release and expand. But if we don't work on allowing the water to support us, swimming can destroy co-ordination. A good example is when learners first attempt to go onto the back from standing, or from tucking up against the wall (see photos). Most people will look for the water with the back of the head, shortening the back of the neck and narrowing the back, instead of allowing the back to uncurl and spread out into the water, below the surface. With the shoulder blades pulled together, the buoyant area where the lungs are can't float. This makes the pelvis and legs heavy. If you tip your head back without giving the water a chance to support your back, your face may sink momentarily and water may go up your nose. This will cause tightening throughout your body and sinking may result (particularly in men).

Above: Regaining feet from back
- Let the head go forward over the feet
- Look at the feet

Right: Going onto the back from the wall - right

Below: Going onto the back from the wall - wrong

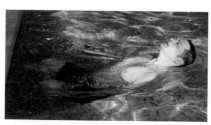

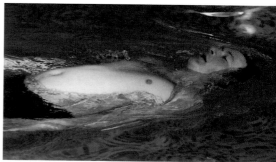

So, to go back onto the back, we need to keep the neck relaxed and extend from the hips, keeping the head, neck and back connected and going all the way back until the water is supporting the head and the whole of the body.

As you swim, keep letting your back spread out into the water and sending your shoulders one away from the other to prevent tension in your chest. Think of your lower spine (the sacrum and coccyx) pointing between your legs, so your pelvis doesn't become heavy (especially important for men). Let the crown of your head lead you backwards as you look up at the ceiling, kicking softly to keep your spine long. It is useful to work on going back into the water and swimming with someone else behind (see photo), who can give you feedback on what is actually happening with your neck and back, even if you are a proficient swimmer.

Co-ordination can be impaired when you swim with fear of taking in water, tire at the end of a swim or struggle to keep up with faster friends in a training session. So remember your head and neck as often as you can. Swimming on your back is a great way to explore quality of movement and balanced rest. It is an opportunity to make expansion and release your goal, to give yourself a break.

Back Stroke - Some common faults and how to avoid them:

Holding the head up in an attempt to avoid getting water over the face.

Let the water support your head throughout the stroke. Don't close your mouth. Allow water into your mouth as a precaution against sniffing it up your nose. The top of your head should lead your spine and the rest of your body through the water.

Rushing the arms

Anxious that the arm coming out of the water will make their head sink, many swimmers stiffen up and try to execute the over water arm action too quickly. The initial anxiety causes the neck and body to stiffen. This makes the arms tight and difficult to control so the arm crashes backwards into the water and the face does sink.

To avoid this downward spiral of events, keep thinking about your head leading, moving away from your spine, and allow your spine to lengthen and your back to widen so that your arm is light and free as you send it skywards. The mark of a good backstroke is a still head and long relaxed arm pointing upwards before resting in the water behind the shoulder. Allow your arm to pause in the air as your hand reaches the furthest point away from you. Then control its quiet descent into the water. Think of your upper arm staying soft as it travels out of the water, floating away from your ribcage. When your hand enters the water, let it rest there for a moment instead of pulling straight away. Enjoy a small glide.

Let your thumb lead your arm out of the water and your little finger lead it back in. Remember to keep your head still but let your body roll, to facilitate an easy entry of your hand that doesn't put strain on your shoulder. When your hand moves out of the water, let your breathing open up as your chest expands.

Practise moving one arm at a time. The sequence is as follows 1. smoothly make an arc with your arm over the water 2. rest your arm in the water behind you, wide of your shoulder 3. move your hand slowly underwater, in an arc, to the side of your body, allowing your elbow to give, and scull sideways to touch your leg with the palm of your hand. Keep kicking for balance and propulsion.

Practise the timing of backstroke arms with six kicks between each stroke, to reinforce the idea of resting the arms. With one hand by your leg and the other in the water behind you, move your arms simultaneously so one is travelling over the water and the other through it.

Kicking from the knees

This makes the legs sink on the downward phase of the kick. It can also create a disturbance at the surface, sending unwanted waves over your face.

Kick from your hips with loose ankles, toes away, so that your feet act like flippers and your legs remain long and don't stray too far from the surface.

Photo © Andy Lane,
courtesy of Steven Shaw.

Try Breaststroke

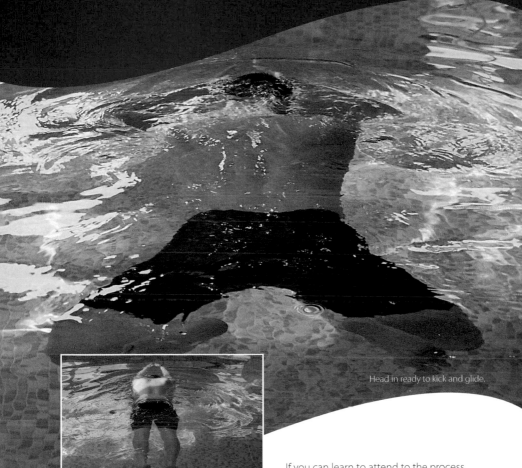

Head in ready to kick and glide.

Glide

Swimming breaststroke can be a great way to improve aerobic fitness, develop muscle tone and enjoy being in the water.

If you can learn to attend to the process of getting your head up to inhale, let your feet do the work and make the glide the foundation of the stroke, breaststroke can be very beneficial for your health.

People new to swimming often find breaststroke easier to swim for sustained periods than front crawl.

But without awareness of what is going on with your head, neck and back, there are potential hazards when swimming this stroke, just as there are with the others.

Building up the breaststroke

Gliding

Before you start swimming breaststroke, be sure you know how to glide, as this stroke is really a series of glides.

The glide is your chance to experience movement without effort and enjoy release of tension and freedom from the task of co-ordinating your limbs.

Stand tall but relaxed before starting to glide. Let your arms float in the water in front of you. Holding them tense is like putting the brakes on. Keep them pointing forward but loose. Think of your shoulders staying soft and going away from each other. Avoid pinching your shoulder blades together.

Keeping your arms away, stay tall as you go silently into the water, breathing gently without taking a deep breath first. Let the crown of your head and your fingers point where you want to go as you look down at the floor.

Push into the floor or wall with your feet and keep breathing out gently until you lose momentum. Don't kick, as the object is to do nothing. Just allow your legs to lengthen, with soft ankles and toes away. Allow your back to be long and wide. Think of your pelvis as part of your back. Breathe gently out into the water throughout. When landing, avoid the tendency to pull your head out of the water first. Instead, watch your knees come forward together, counterbalance with your arms moving back and raise your head only when your feet are planted on the floor. Think of going down to land, not getting up for air.

Breaststroke kick

The main propulsive agent in the breaststroke is the kick. Maintaining quietness in your neck, head and back, which you have achieved in the glide, add the froglike breaststroke kick.

The crown of your head should point forwards to the end of the pool as you extend your legs in the other direction. For a froglike kick, let the feet turn outwards as you gently bend at your hips, allowing your knees to come forward and away from each other. Think of your feet drifting away from each other as your legs bend. Keep this movement as slow as you can - avoid *pulling* your knees up. Let your lower spine lengthen as your legs bend - avoid hollowing your lower back. Pause, with your feet turned out and soles pointing back and down, ready for the kick. Then extend your legs backwards and outwards, with your feet moving away from each other, before accelerating as they come together to create a glide. This propulsive phase of the kick is a semi-circular motion. Think of drawing a circle with your feet.

Look at hands.

Breaststroke arm action

The breaststroke arm action helps you get your face out of the water to inhale before working with your legs to create a glide. Most people have a strong, instinctive tendency to pull their arms all the way back to the hips. This movement may serve you well when swimming underwater but it hinders the process of coming out to inhale.

The arm movement should consist of a gentle scull with your hands, followed by a pointing, gliding motion. From the glide, slowly let your hands come apart, a little further than shoulder width, palms facing down. Think of your back staying wide. Pause here. Now, instead of turning your palms backwards to pull yourself through the water, point your fingers down then turn your palms up and bring your little fingers together as your hands meet under your chin. Avoid pulling your elbows into your sides and keep space around your shoulders and armpits so that the sculling action takes place in front of your body. Think of your upper arms staying forward, in front of your shoulders, and away from each other. When this gentle scull is completed, extend your arms into a glide and rest them out in front. Avoid the often-irresistible urge to go straight into another pull.

Timing of arms and legs

Work on co-ordinating the arm and leg movements before attempting to come up to inhale. Think of making a circle with your hands followed by a circle with your feet. From the glide, first let your hands move apart. This movement is important because, if you remember to do it, it prevents the instinctive pulling movement described earlier and keeps your hands in front of you where they need to be. Next, as you scull with your hands meeting underneath your face, let your feet drift very slowly forwards. You have now drawn a circle with your hands. The arms and legs are

Top: Watch hands open.
Next: Raise head to breathe, scull with hands as legs bend.

both bent, in preparation for extension. As you extend your arms into a glide, you can accelerate as you draw the circle with your feet. Your arms are out in front as your feet come together with legs straight, ankles relaxed and toes pointed. You can now enjoy gliding in this fully elongated position. When working on the timing of arms and legs, think of pointing your arms to set you up for the kick and glide. You may consider the circular scull of your hands simply to be preparation for pointing them for the all-important glide.

Coming up to inhale

When swimming breaststroke, there are two separate agendas, which you must keep separate in your mind. **Agenda one** is to get your head up to inhale. This is followed by a kick and glide, to move forward, which is **agenda two**. Many people make themselves move forward, by pulling their arms all the way back to the hips, at the same time as attempting to lift the head to breathe. This creates confusion in the body and strain in the neck and back.

Because of anxiety about breathing, many people put all their effort into this phase of the stroke with nothing much happening to create forward movement when the head returns to the water. A pupil of mine described her old breaststroke as "bobbing up and down like a demented cork"!

We need to learn a counter-intuitive movement pattern for breaststroke breathing, to prevent the strain of raising the head in an instinctive, fearful way. It makes for a calm, unforced inhalation instead of a rushed gasp.

To get your head out of the water to inhale without strain, your head itself needs to lead, with your arms providing assistance. Instead of forcing your head out by shortening the middle of your back, the task is to employ the joint at the top of your spine, in between your ears, where the skull articulates with the top vertebra (atlanto-occipital joint). To avoid strain, you need to explore the range of movement available at this joint. Standing on dry land, follow your eyes to look at the ceiling, without leading with your chin. Instead of collapsing your spine to do this, keep your back long and wide. Bringing your head back against a lively, open back is the movement you need for breaststroke breathing.

From the glide, take your time to look at your hands resting together in front of you. Think of your spine lengthening right down to the tail as you enjoy the movement at the atlanto-occipital joint to bring your head back, following your eyes. When you can see your hands, pause to watch them come gently apart. You can now see them out of the corners of your eyes. Your arms should still be straight. Now move your head again, eyes breaking the surface, followed by nose and mouth, as you continue breathing out. Your hands then scull underneath your face, to help maintain this head position.

Here, with your elbows wide and your back open, all the conditions are right for a nice in-breath. When swimming, remember to focus on the out-breath and let the in-breath do itself.

Practise this set of movements standing in the water. Be aware that the head always moves before the hands:

Look at your hands before watching them open. Move your head out of the water before sculling. Release your head into the water before sending your hands forwards.

Putting it all together

Start with a relaxed glide, always breathing out gently underwater.

Agenda 1: As your head comes out of the water for the in-breath, as described above, let your feet drift forwards. Avoid *pulling* your feet toward you, a movement which is linked to *pulling* the head out. Think of keeping both movements soft and gentle. These two movements should be connected through the lengthening spine. Looking ahead, with your chin remaining in the water, let the air in. Then let your face return underwater, look at the floor, and allow the back of your neck and the whole of your spine to lengthen. Extend your arms in front, ready for the forward movement.

Agenda 2: Don't execute the propulsive phase of the kick - the circular, backward, outward and together phase - until you have released your head into the water.

Focus on enjoying the non-doing glide phase and you can't go wrong.

Swim Like a Fish
Front Crawl Part 1

Do some swimmers leave you, working your socks off, in their wake as they glide effortlessly into the distance? If so, you need to focus on gliding, releasing and lengthening in front crawl. Top swimmers do this but it doesn't come naturally to most of us. Unnecessary tension impedes *feel* for water so relaxation is the key to good front crawl. This lesson won't cover front crawl breathing but don't forget to keep gently exhaling when your face is in the water. Never hold your breath or force air out.

Work on technique over fitness

In your swimming sessions, are you using your crawl to work harder and harder in the wrong direction i.e. reinforcing bad habits instead of improving technique?

If you don't work on your stroke, benefits gained from increasing fitness will be negligible against the amount of effort you put in. Mental application will do more for your swimming than working your body like a slave. Terry Laughlin [1], a major US triathlon swimming coach, has an unconventional view on swimming fitness: it happens when you work on technique.

"The only truly effective way to become a better swimmer is to approach every swim workout as primarily a nervous system training session and let your aerobic training become an incidental effect of cumulative hours you spend in the pool working on greater stroke efficiency."

Reducing strokes per length

When swimming, there is an instinctive tendency to keep the body square in the water and move forwards only by *pulling* with the arms. Instinctive movements never work in the water. The science of greater stroke efficiency is based on the fact that "a long boat is faster than a short boat". Fast swimmers achieve efficiency by gliding through the water with each stroke, as well as pulling. So the most important skill to develop is gliding on your side. Laughlin calls this non-instinctive movement "fishlike swimming".

True length in the crawl is not achieved by over-stretching the shoulder but by rolling the hips and using the length of the whole body as well as the extended arm. Think of the arm's extension beginning at your hip and enjoy the flow of your body moving easily through the water. Teachers who use the principles of the Alexander Technique help swimmers to enjoy the non-doing aspect of all strokes[2]. While this style of swimming is similar to that described by coaches like Laughlin, the emphasis is on improving the quality of the experience rather than swimming faster. By letting go of tension caused by a desire to swim fast, we will become more efficient and develop a feel for water. We can increase our potential to swim faster without trying.

Learning side balance

It is useful to break strokes down into their fundamental components and practise these. To help you become comfortable with front crawl gliding, travel forward with your head still, eyes down, releasing the side of your lengthening body into the water, with one arm extended in front, thumb up, the other resting at your side. Kick from your hips, loose ankles and toes away, with legs facing the wall not the floor. This angle of your body and legs will feel strange at first. Kick six times, gently exhaling, then stop. When this feels easy, change sides by taking one stroke, keeping your head still, and continue kicking to maintain the new glide.

In front crawl, if you don't vary the angle of your legs when kicking but keep them facing the floor, with hips fixed, you will prevent a full glide and cause strain in the middle of your back when you roll your shoulders. Kicking is more about balance and continuity of the forward direction of head and spine, than propulsion.

Timing and tempo of the arms

To make gliding possible in front crawl, don't pull your arm back as soon as it enters the water. Instead, enter the water thumb side first then let your arm spiral forward so your arm glides thumb side up and your hip rolls to accommodate more glide. With your thumbs up, your arms are lighter and your back is more open.

One arm should always be extended forward and gliding. The glide continues as the other arm recovers over the water so that, for much of the stroke, two arms are directed forward at the same time. During the whole of the recovery over the water, you want to be getting the most out of the forward arm glide. You can think of the recovering arm almost catching up with the forward arm.

A light and free extended forward arm facilitates the easy recovery of the other arm by helping to maintain side balance. One arm gliding as the other recovers over the water is a key moment in the front crawl stroke. The recovering arm falls upwards out of the water, staying relaxed, using the momentum from the accelerated scull to the hip. This sculling movement (see next page) also gives acceleration to the glide of the forward arm. To help with this timing, notice the moment when your hands are spread apart, one forward, one back, thumbs up, enabling space across the chest.

Don't let your elbow leave the water first. This shortens your stroke and causes stiffness in your shoulder. Let your hand leave first, thumb side up, and point to the ceiling. The high bent elbow, which facilitates the hip roll, can be achieved naturally when you release the hand and forearm towards the water for entry.

Focus on timing, not the specifics of the underwater arm action.

The sculling movement, referred to in the previous page, which happens at the end of the underwater journey of the arm, is your reward for not trying to pull too early. If you try to *do* something to "catch" the water, your hand may slip ineffectually through it. But if you wait and continue to direct your arm forward for long enough, you may enjoy the sensation of getting

hold of the water and moving yourself along, as if holding on to a handle, when you scull towards your hip. Think of the underwater phase of your arm making an arc which goes slightly outside your body rather than underneath it. This enables you to keep your back wide and shoulders soft. If your timing is right, you should get hold of the water enough to create a new glide. The arms work together as a unit, with the whole body involved in the length and power of the stroke. Power from the hips is emphasised in tennis, martial arts and golf but often underestimated in swimming.

Keep your head still

When you roll your body from side to side, your head may also want to turn. Remember to keep your neck free, lead with the crown of the head and let your spine lengthen. Let your hips and shoulders roll, keeping your back in one piece. Stillness and constant forward direction of head and spine are a prerequisite of smooth swimming. Focusing only on the propulsive action of your arms and legs makes for a disconnected and untidy stroke.

Swim quietly

Don't make a big splash when getting your hand out of water – it might feel good but it achieves nothing. Don't make entering the water with your hand a big event. You don't need to make an effort to get your hand through the surface.

Switch from left to right

Remember to keep your left arm to the left of your head and spine, right arm to the right. In other words, as you roll from side to side, take care not to overdo it, which results in narrowing your back and forcing your shoulder blades together. Your hand should enter in front of your shoulder. Keep space between your shoulders. Take your hand out of the water in front of your hip. Going behind your hip will tighten your back and disturb your balance. Standing in water, watch the movement of your arms, to improve timing and technique. Imagine swimming along railway tracks, not a monorail. Staying wide is as important as keeping your length.

Keep your shoulders soft throughout the stroke. It is very easy to misuse shoulders when swimming. The shoulder is a flexible but unstable part of the anatomy, easily prone to injury. Swimmer's shoulder is an avoidable complaint but there is a high incidence of shoulder surgery among competitive swimmers.

Final thought

The approach most common to fitness swimmers and triathletes is to try hard, grind muscles and move limbs as fast as possible. All this gets us nowhere. What really makes us move is forward direction coming out of ease in and oneness with the water. If you make this your goal in front crawl, it will get better. Even if you're not up there with the elite, you should have some energy left when you get out of the water.

(1)   The Guide to Fishlike Swimming, Terry Laughlin, Total Immersion Swiminar Workbook, 1996.

(2)   See The Art of Swimming – a new direction using the Alexander Technique, Steven Shaw and Armand D'Angour, Ashgrove, 1996.

Enjoy Breathing
Front Crawl Part 2

Breathe out gently underwater. Keep breathing out until *you* are out. Then let the in-breath happen on its own, don't force it.

In the last lesson, we looked at swimming front crawl without turning to breathe - kicking on the side, gliding, with the front arm extended as the other arm recovers light and free over the water, and rolling from side to side, with the head leading and spine lengthening. In this lesson, we continue with one of the most challenging swimming skills, turning to inhale without panicking, hyperventilating or sucking in water.

Are you rushing the process?

A good question to ask yourself about your front crawl breathing is could you stop at any point in the stroke, rest the arms and continue moving forward by kicking? In other words, is the water supporting you while you turn to breathe or are you going off balance to do it?

Most people can co-ordinate front crawl fairly naturally. They would be ok if it wasn't for the breathing. When it comes to getting the head out to breathe, people usually learn it on a trial and error basis until they get the knack. At the learning stage, you will see people contorting their face, twisting their neck, lifting their head away from the surface and gasping as though this breath could be their last. You may also observe that the stroke momentarily comes to a halt as the desire to get a breath takes over – the forward motion is lost and the stroke deteriorates. This fear response is natural. The problem is that even when you are confident that you can gain an in-breath whenever required, habit and lack of awareness may cause these fearful movements to persist.

Most front crawl learners will encounter the nasty sensation of swallowing chlorinated water, or sniffing it into the sinuses. When the learner finds a way of making sure this does not happen, it is only natural to carry on breathing in this, relatively successful, way. But just because you don't swallow water any more, it doesn't mean you're getting it right or all the anxiety has gone away. If there is any anxiety at all about whether you are going to get air in and avoid swallowing water, the movement pattern you use is likely to put you under more pressure by limiting the time you've got. In other words, you're going to rush the process. Anxiety about getting a breath leads to a decision to try harder. This causes unnecessary tension in the neck and back

and loss of balance in and support from the water. This hinders breathing and disturbs the rhythm of the stroke.

Resting with your face out

The solution to this common problem will, for most people, lead to a whole new experience of front crawl, where turning to breathe is an integral part of the stroke. It can be an activity that substitutes release for stiffness of the neck, lengthening for shortening of the spine, an open chest for a tight one and calm breathing for hyperventilation.

The aim is to learn not how to get a breath but to be balanced and supported by the water in the breathing position. In the last lesson we looked at kicking on the side with the face in, one arm extended, legs at an angle to the floor. For breathing, we need to practise this skill but with the face out of the water. When first attempting this, the instinctive tendency is to stiffen the neck and lift the head away from the support of the water. When on the side, lifting the head like this actually pushes the jaw, mouth and nose under the surface and makes the hips sink.

Letting the heavy upper part of your head float should ensure that your mouth and nose are clear of the surface. You also need to make sure the extended forward arm is free and directed out of your body, pointing where you want to go, and the side of your body is supported and lengthening. Swimming is easier when you release your head and allow your hips to float higher.

So kick on your side with your face out of the water but head releasing into it. To start with, look up to the ceiling, similar to the head position for backstroke. With more practice, you can find a sideways resting position for your head, one ear in, and one out. Practise this activity on its own until you can move easily in this position, with your neck free and back open and without holding your breath. It will feel alien at first so give it time.

To recap

- Keep your neck soft.
- Don't over stretch the forward arm but let it extend from your hip and keep it pointing forward, in the same direction as the crown of your head.
- Keep reminding yourself to let your head be supported by the water, against the instinctive tendency to hold it up.
- Kick continuously with loose ankles and toes away.
- Don't hold your breath.
- Don't arch your back. Keep it long and wide.

Freedom to have a breather

When you are happy swimming on your side with your face out of the water, all you have to do to inhale in front crawl is get into this familiar and comfortable position. There is a huge psychological difference between turning quickly in order to get a breath, where you may strain your body, and turning almost for the sake of turning, to get into a situation where you feel relaxed and can keep moving forward for as long as you like. Inhaling can then be leisurely, almost incidental; it can happen on its own instead of being forced. The important thing to remember is to keep pointing yourself, and moving, forward. Swim with your face in, always gently letting air out, rolling from

side to side, with your head still, and when you decide to turn to breathe, simply let your head follow the spiral of your body and momentum of your underwater arm. Keep rolling until your head is resting with your face out of the water and don't try to breathe in until you are resting. In other words, keep breathing out until *you* are out. In time this can all happen in an instant so that the rhythm of the stroke is undisturbed. But to start with, be prepared to stay in the position, as if resting from the stroke but kicking to maintain momentum, until you have breathed in naturally and feel ready to return. Think of turning to have a breather instead of taking a breath.

Don't lose your forward arm

When you begin to practise front crawl breathing, you need to pause in the breathing position, maintaining side balance and releasing your head. Otherwise, not only will a relaxed in-breath be difficult, you will also be likely to *lose* your forward arm. In the last lesson we looked at the instinctive tendency to pull the arms back too early and the importance of the forward arm glide. If you rush the breathing and lift your head, your arm will move back through the water too early and there will be no glide. So think of your arm pointing where you want to go as you roll to breathe and kick continuously.

Freedom to have a breather.

Returning to swim with your face in

When returning your face to the water, leave the forward arm in front for as long as possible and glide. This is, firstly, to maintain side balance as the opposite arm recovers and, secondly, so you can use it to get you moving forward again as the opposite arm replaces it and glides.

Watch the other arm recover, thumb first, light and free, as you direct it towards the sky. This movement encourages opening of the chest and this is the natural moment for the in-breath to happen. As your elbow bends and your recovering arm releases towards the water, let your head return and then change your arms. The arm that has been extended in front can now create more glide for its partner as it sculls toward the hip.

In the same way that the arm coming up out of the water opens the chest for the in-breath, when it goes into the water and extends, this encourages the out- breath.

This can be easily demonstrated on dry land. Stand with your arms by your side, right foot forward. Take your left arm back to point behind you. Notice how this encourages an in breath. Now swing it forward as you step forward with your left leg and see how this encourages an out-breath.

Final thought

Be prepared to take time to change your front crawl, or to learn this style of swimming. Remember your goal is to improve your relationship with the water. More and more instinctive swimming, without awareness of what you're actually doing, won't help you achieve this and will limit development of your technique.

Returning to swim with the face in.

Think Before You Swim

Letting the water support your head as you inhale allows you to keep your back open and makes for a more relaxed stroke.

Ten common misconceptions to consider.

1. Swimming is injury free

It is surprisingly easy to injure yourself by swimming with inappropriate technique. There is a high incidence of shoulder and knee injuries among competitive swimmers, often resulting in surgery.

If there is any anxiety about the process of breathing, you are likely to strain your neck and back and give yourself headaches.

2. I'm a sinker

Men in particular often believe they can't float because they have been taught to aim for horizontality, e.g. to make star shapes. So long as your head floats when you are face down and motionless, it doesn't matter if the rest of you sinks. Gentle kicking will help keep your legs afloat.

We swim *in* the water, not *on* it. Tensing yourself up to try to stay on the surface will be disastrous for your swimming and, for triathletes, will lead to exhaustion before the cycle and run. Relaxation is the key to buoyancy.

3. I've got to take a deep breath

You need no more air in your lungs before putting your head in the water for a swimming stroke than for speaking a sentence or blowing your nose. Many novice swimmers hyperventilate by focusing on the in-breath and not letting enough air out into the water. If you gently make bubbles under water and continue breathing out as you come up for air, the in-breath should take care of itself. If you can hear yourself sucking air in, you're probably overdoing it. Avoid forcing too much air out by pursing your lips and *blowing* bubbles.

Any "correct" head position that you try to put into practice is likely to cause tension in your neck.

Photo © Spencer Duval.

4. I should make an 's-pattern' with my hand underwater

Many swimming and triathlon manuals talk about an 's-pattern' in front crawl. Steven Shaw says it is a "recipe for scoliosis". Your brain can only cope with so many movement-related thoughts at once. If you are too specific with your thinking about the trajectory of your hand underwater, you may lose the sense of the whole stroke. After winning one of the races on his way to seven Olympic gold medals, Mark Spitz was asked what he was doing underwater. He believed himself to be simply 'catching' the water by bending his elbow and then moving his hand in a straight line to his hip. But underwater analysis proved there was a series of zigzag movements, now known as an 's-pattern'. While the camera never lies, would-be Mark Spitzes attempting to recreate his stroke would do better to follow the thoughts actually guiding his movements. Think of the catch phase as a gentle, non-doing movement, and use the hip roll with the sculling motion of your hand towards your hip to create forward motion.

5. The water line should be in the middle of my forehead.

Any "correct" head position that you try to put into practice is likely to cause tension in your neck. The most useful thought about head position is that you should let the water take the weight of your head so you are not pulling your head back against your spine and shortening your neck and back. If you attend to this, you will find you are looking down at the floor.

6. Every session should include a kicking and pulling set

Holding a kickboard creates tension in your neck, shoulders and back. It also keeps your hips in an artificial, flat position. In front crawl you need to roll your body and allow the angle of your legs to change constantly. So it makes more sense to practise kicking on your side (see lesson 4). Likewise, using a pull-buoy can lead to faulty technique because it fixes your hips in a square position and prevents the long stroke which comes from rolling your body. Every pull should be carried out in conjunction with a gliding motion of your other arm. (see lesson 4) It is difficult to achieve this when using a pull buoy.

7. I don't need goggles

Goggles are essential for clear vision and orientation and stop chlorinated water from stinging your eyes. All these things lead to more confidence and relaxation so goggles that work for you are second in importance only to a swimsuit, and only just!

8. No pain, no gain

This is the main idea that gets fitness swimmers and triathletes into trouble. Training harder and harder for better results without addressing problems in your technique is particularly harmful for your swimming. For triathletes, it is also essential to check out your running and cycling technique. Think technique and injury prevention first, fitness second.

9. Practice makes perfect

"When at first you don't succeed, never try again, at least, not in the same way. Trying almost always involves extra and excessive tension" Patrick MacDonald [1]

Practising sloppy technique reinforces it. Remember that winners of swimming races always take fewest strokes per length. Efficiency is crucial for triathletes, who need to conserve energy for the cycle and run.

10. Weight training will improve my swimming

Many people use weights, in a belief that this will help prevent injury. Most swimming injuries arise as a result of over training and, particularly for inexperienced swimmers, inappropriate technique and/or faulty patterns of co-ordination. No amount of weight training will help prevent these injuries. Injuries are your body's way of telling you to stop doing what you're doing and alter your technique by redirecting your attention.

(1)   Patrick MacDonald, The Alexander Technique as I See It; Rahula, 1989.

Holding your head up to inhale causes strain in the neck and back and makes the stroke less efficient. The water should be supporting your head even when you inhale.

Photo © Spencer Duval.

Kitting Yourself Out

One of the beauties of swimming is the very limited amount of equipment you need. There is a handful of real essentials for your swimming bag, some products that may enhance your training if used appropriately and others better avoided.

✓ Swimsuit

If you are training in chlorinated water, the first essential is a suit made of chlorine resistant material. Anything made with around 50% PBT will last at least 20 times longer than conventionally made swimsuits, for less than twice the price. Men's briefs start at around £17, women's suits at around £25. I recommend the Speedo Endurance range.

✓ Goggles

Goggles are a must for training in the pool. Water distorts vision and pool water may sting your eyes. To be able to open the eyes freely underwater and see properly is important for orientation, balance and calmness when swimming. It is worth paying at least £10 for goggles that are easy to adjust and comfortable. Frames made of soft plastic, which sit outside your eye-socket, provide most comfort. All goggles start misting up after a while so, for prolonged anti-fog protection, it is worth buying some spray (around £4). When goggles mist up during a swim, dip them in the water. Don't rub the lens with your fingers. Increasingly popular among triathletes are swimming masks (from £15), with 180 degrees panoramic vision and excellent suction. Masks are a great improvement on goggles in open water but work equally well in the pool. Many goggles and masks are available with tinted or photochromic lenses for outdoor use. I recommend the Aqua Sphere range. See shop.swimmingwithoutstress.co.uk

✓ Wetsuit

A wetsuit is a close fitting neoprene (man made rubber) suit that lets water in through openings such as the neck, not through the neoprene itself. The water settles between the skin and the neoprene and body warmth heats up the water, keeping you warm. For the system to work, the wetsuit needs to be well made and close fitting. Studies have shown that less experienced swimmers produce faster times when wearing a wetsuit. If you are planning to take part in an open water triathlon event in the UK, a wetsuit is compulsory.

Go for one thin enough not to restrict your movement. Thick, warm wetsuits designed for surfing or diving will impede movement and make you so buoyant that you struggle to find your swimming stroke. A wetsuit designed for swimming will be thin enough to move freely in, while giving you just enough extra buoyancy and warmth. Swimming wetsuits cost between £80 and £100 and should be adequate for the needs of most triathletes. Specially designed triathlon wetsuits made by top brands will cost in excess of £200. The benefits are extreme closeness of fit, excellent flexibility for the arms and designs to facilitate quick removal. You should expect your wetsuit to be very tight fitting across the chest. If your suit feels too tight for you to move on dry land, you can expect this to change in the water. A wetsuit that feels comfortable on land is probably too big and will let in too much water. If possible, buy from a specialist, or try on with the help of an experienced user, who can advise you.

✓ Swim cap

When you are swimming in open water, a silicone cap (around £5) or two will help to keep you warm. When training in pools, on the other hand, a cap stops you from experiencing the true buoyancy of your head and can make you feel too hot, possibly causing headaches. A new style of swimming hat, the Aqua Sphere Glide (around £10) has been specially designed to fit comfortably over the ears and may make your open water swim more comfortable.

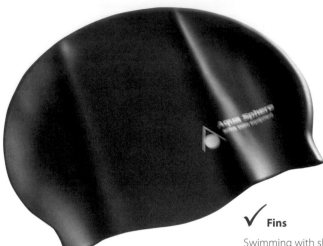

✗ Kickboard

Most competitive swimmers train with a kickboard, a flat piece of foam with a couple of holes for handles. Conventional opinion is that each training session should include a kicking set of up to 400 metres, to isolate and strengthen leg muscles and improve kicking technique. The alternative view is that holding the kickboard locks up the arms and shoulders. Most swimmers also keep the head out of the water while kicking with a kickboard, putting strain on the neck and back. The other disadvantage is that you are training your hips to remain in a false square position. In the full stroke your hips need to roll, with the angle of your legs changing as your whole body rolls from side to side. You can practise kicking by working on the side with one arm extended (see front crawl lessons). Think carefully about using a kickboard just because so many other people do.

✓ Water-bottle

Don't forget to keep taking sips of water. You will dehydrate quickly in swimming pools, even when you are not exercising.

✓ Fins

Swimming with short fins designed for swim training is an excellent way to improve your kick. The key to kicking technique is loose ankles and flipper like feet. The range of any joint is greater in water. The ankle is a hinge joint and in front crawl kicking you should get a real feeling of the hinge working. The ankle flexibility that good kicking technique gives you is useful for runners, who are often tight in this area. Wearing fins trains you to let your feet act as flippers and, when you take them off, the new movement continues. I recommend using fins for short distances, just to get a feel for the flipper movement. It is also fun to experience the inevitable increase in speed they will give you.

✗ Pull buoy

This figure-of-eight shaped piece of foam is a very popular tool for keeping the legs afloat while you isolate the arms. However, with your head releasing into the water, the crown of your head leading and with good forward direction through the spine and the gliding arm, you should be able to rest your legs without needing a pull buoy. The trouble with a pull buoy is that it fixes your hips in a square position. By encouraging the swimmer to pull with the arms, at the expense of using the roll of the hip, it creates an unnatural twist in the spine. For this reason, it is not recommended.

✓ Earplugs

There is a danger of picking up an ear infection if you get water stuck inside your ear, particularly if swimming in open water. The first thing to look at, if this is happening, is your head position. If you bury your head too deep into the water, for instance, you may be forcing water into your ears. But if the problem occurs frequently, earplugs are very useful. I would avoid wax or silicone plugs which you can mould to the shape of your ear. They tend to fall out and get dirty very easily. Plastic earplugs last for years and seem to repel dirt. Tree shaped plastic earplugs are uncomfortable as they have to be screwed well into the ear. My favourite kind of earplug is shaped to fit securely inside the ear without feeling too intrusive. Expect to pay around £3 for a pair. Wearing these earplugs, you should still be able to hold a conversation.

✗ Nose clip

Your nose is for breathing. To shut it off with a nose clip in order to avoid sniffing in water is not the answer to difficulties with front crawl breathing. Learn to exhale through your nose. You may even choose to learn to breathe in through your nose. This is not conventional swimming technique but breathing in through the mouth is not after all what nature intended.

✓ Foot spray

If you are prone to fungal infections of the skin on your feet, there are excellent sprays to keep the soles of your feet silky smooth! A consultation with a podiatrist may be worthwhile. Products available only from podiatrists are more effective than those you can buy off the shelf from chemists. Be prepared to pay around £5 per 100 ml.

✓ Videos for Technique

Aleksandre Popov: What's the Limit? Sprint Freestyle is very useful for anyone wanting to learn or improve front crawl technique (around £26). In the Shaw Method Steps video (£11), Steven Shaw guides you through a series of clear steps to help you learn or improve front crawl, breast stroke and backstroke.

✓ Oh, and don't forget your towel!

But as Popov himself said, when asked if he would be wearing a body suit to shave milliseconds off his time in the Sydney Olympic Games, "The water is your friend. Treat it kindly and it will help you move." In other words, all the help you really need is in the water itself.

Interval Training

For aerobic fitness improvement, a better sense of your own pace and the opportunity to attend to technique, try interval training.

What is Interval Training?

Interval training involves splitting your total training distance into a chosen number of smaller distances, aiming to complete these distances in a target time, and including a period of rest in between each distance.

A group of distances and target times, including rests in between, is called a set.

The target distances and times will often be the same throughout the set. In this case, the distance within a set is called a repeat. Here is an example of one such set, which will form part of a training session. Swim 100 metres (normally 4 lengths) with a target time of 2 minutes. Repeat 4 times with 20 seconds rest in between each repeat. This can be represented in your training plan like this:

5x 100metres @2mins on 2.20mins

During interval training, rests should be short in relation to the time set for the repeat- between 1/12 of the time (e.g. 10 seconds rest when swimming 100 metres in 2 minutes) and 1/3 (e.g. 2 minutes rest when swimming 400 metres in 6 minutes). During your rest the aim should be to recover partially, i.e. let the heart rate and breathing rate slow down without returning to their normal, resting rate. In this way, the rest is actually part of your aerobic workout. If, during the swim repeat, your heart rate was 150 bpm then during the recovery it may go down to 120 bpm.

Each training session should consist of a warm up, one to three of these sets and a cool down. Please read lessons on front crawl in Part One and be prepared to break down the strokes to work on technique during your warm up and cool down and between sets. Working on technique should be the main focus of any swim training session.

What are the benefits of this kind of training?

Judging your pace

Interval training develops your ability to judge your pace and to swim within your aerobic capacity. This is very important in a triathlon race. You want to avoid starting out too fast and exhausting yourself for the cycle and run or, worse, making it difficult to complete the swim. Suppose your race included a 500-metre swim and it took you 10 minutes, with the first 100 metres completed in 1 minute and 45 seconds, the third 100 metres in 2 minutes and the fifth in 2 minutes and 15 seconds. You started too fast and ended up struggling. Your technique suffered as you worked hard to complete the distance and this further decreased your speed and sapped you of your energy for the cycle and run.

More satisfactory and a better triathlon racing strategy would be a smoother 10-minute swim, with even 100 metre splits of 2 minutes, and consistent technique. (For feedback regarding what is happening with your technique, try counting strokes per length). If this is achievable, in your interval training you would aim to swim a little faster - 5 x 100 metres @1 minute, 50 seconds, with 10 seconds rest between each repeat, also written like this:

5 x 100m @ 1.50 on 2 mins.

To give another example, in your training you decide to swim 4 x 200 metres. A 60/70% perceived effort rate or a heart rate of around 140 to 150 bpm during your first 200-metre swim produces the time of 3 minutes 30 seconds. This feels easy but your aim is to repeat this another three times: 4 x 200m @ 3:30 on 4:30 (1 min rest between sets).

If you can't, you swam the first 200-metre repeat too fast. You are learning what it feels like to swim at a certain speed and maintain that speed. It is especially important in triathlon training and racing to swim times that are right for you. Measure your heart rate and/or give an honest assessment of your own effort rate. You will do yourself no favours struggling to keep up with other swimmers who are technically better, fitter and faster than you. You must be realistic in both training and races or you will get injured in training or struggle to complete an unsatisfactory race.

A chance to stop

One great advantage of interval training is that during rests you can calm down, let your neck be free and enjoy the body's state of high activity without needing to think about co-ordinating the strokes. Remind yourself you are a land animal, find your feet on the ground, and let your head lead you upwards and your spine lengthen. Try to breathe through your nose. All this is important as, if you collapse and grasp the side of the pool, as many do, you won't get the most from your rest. After swimming you need to regain your vertical poise. I would say to triathletes, if, after swimming any distance, you don't have the energy to stand up, you are not preparing yourself well for a long cycle and run!

Resting also allows you to evaluate your swimming technique. As you stand and give attention to yourself, is anything hurting, and if so, can you work out why? There's

always a reason and it's usually to do with inappropriate actions in your stroke. You can use the rest time to plan keeping your stroke long, by rolling the hips and gliding, and balanced, by keeping the left arm left of your head and spine and right arm right, for example. Keeping the hips square and twisting the neck to breathe can cause headaches. Too narrow an entry point for the hands will cause tightness in the shoulders and possibly injury. In triathlon races, you need to feel free in the joints when getting out of the water. You want to get on the bike with light arms and soft shoulders. Be careful not to destroy your co-ordination in the water before beginning the other two thirds of the race.

Swimming faster

With interval training you can practise swimming faster while staying within your aerobic limits. In a triathlon race, adrenaline will give you a surprising helping hand, particularly as swimming is the first leg. You may find yourself swimming your normal interval times, which your body is used to, but without the need for the rests. For example, you've practised swimming 100 metres @ 1 m 30 seconds on 2 minutes and in a race, to your amazement, you can swim 800 metres close to 12 minutes.

Fun and motivation

Creating a variety of interval training sets makes swimming challenging and fun. There should always be plenty to keep your mind occupied anyway, as your primary focus in every swim should be improving technique. Remember US triathlon coach Terry Laughlin's idea:

"The only truly effective way to become a better swimmer is to approach every swim workout as primarily a nervous system training session and let your aerobic training become an incidental effect of cumulative hours you spend in the pool working on greater stroke efficiency."

However, if you're swimming for fitness or preparing for a triathlon race, planning interval training sessions is a great way to motivate yourself, learn about your potential and keep you focused on your goals. Keep a training log but do beware of becoming a slave to the clock!

To sum up, Interval Training...

1. improves aerobic fitness

2. helps you judge your effort and speed

3. helps you monitor your fitness level

4. makes you swim faster

5. provides the opportunity for rest and evaluation of technique

6. adds fun and creativity to your sessions

7. helps you to cover greater distances without getting too tired and to train aerobically for longer

8. helps prevent sloppy technique

9. motivates you to train

10. makes it easy to log your progress

10 Tips for Interval Training

1 Use the pool clock if there is one. This is the easiest way to check how you're doing and to make sure you set off at the planned time. Using a stopwatch can be useful but avoid becoming obsessed with times. You may need to be flexible about departure times if there are other people in your lane. Be prepared to abandon monitoring times and use perceived effort rate and heart rate instead.

2 Make sure you have a water bottle at the poolside and take sips as often as you can. Because of the heat around you, it is very easy to dehydrate but being in cold water can stop you feeling thirsty.

3 Check your heart rate regularly. For a quick check, count the pulse on your throat for 6 seconds and multiply by 10. Aim to stay between 120 and 160 beats per minute (bpm) for aerobic training.

4 Know your limits – you are aiming to improve your technique and fitness gently. Focus on your own development instead of trying to keep up with other, faster swimmers.

5 Find a training partner of similar ability– this will help you stay motivated.

6 Keep a logbook – you can record times, perceived effort rates, heart rates and discoveries about technique. This gives you a true record of your progress and helps keep you motivated.

7 Aim for poise, not collapse, during rests. Be aware of your neck and allow your back to lengthen and widen as you find your feet on the floor. Think of space between your shoulders. Breathe through the nose.

8 Don't lose your technique in an effort to swim faster. Keep working to let go of unnecessary tension and to reduce strokes per length.

9 Put your training schedule inside a plastic transparent file pocket and keep it at the side of the pool.

10 Allow plenty of time for each session. Always include a warm up, specific work on technique and cool down. If you need to shorten your training session to save time, don't sacrifice technique. For example, here is a 20- minute lunch-time session (650 metres) which should set you up for a good afternoon.

1. Release, expand and calm down by gliding and floating supine (5 minutes)
2. Swim 100 metres easy, working on front crawl side balance and swimming on your back (3 minutes)
3. Swim 400 metre easy front crawl with even 100 metre 'splits', e.g. 2 minutes per 100 metres (8 minutes)
4. Rest and let your neck be free (30 seconds)
5. Swim 150 metres slowly including backstroke and breaststroke, enjoying the glide (3 minute 30 seconds)

Alternative Triathlon Training

Be a Zen Triathlete

Fitness can damage your health[1]. While aerobic fitness is an important facet of health, it is all too easy to over train, especially in a sport like triathlon. To achieve and maintain an optimum level of fitness you don't need to work unreasonably hard.

Professional athletes are aerobically super fit: they have very low resting heart rates, quick recovery after exertion, great lung capacity and muscle tone. But people doing a very high level of training are not always the healthiest.

Serious athletes often struggle to shake off illness. Because their training programmes don't allow sufficient rest, they will often continue training before properly recovering from viruses. This may lead to them either getting more seriously ill or becoming more and more lethargic until their training regime eventually breaks down. Many athletes constantly battle against injuries. When your livelihood is at stake, you can't afford to take it easy: you have to push yourself to the limits. But if this is happening to you, you need to think about what you really want from your sport.

Most triathletes set out looking for a new challenge. They want to enjoy training in three disciplines, getting fitter and competing in races. Unfortunately it is very easy to get sucked into the negative aspects of competition. Once we start pushing ourselves too hard and training becomes out of proportion to the rest of our lives, we are heading for injury, frustration and finally burnout. There is a danger for all athletes of being super fit one minute and sedentary the next. Triathlon training can be a long-term part of your healthy lifestyle. But, just like in a race, you have to pace yourself.

Healthy triathlon training needs the following three elements:

Sensible aims

Why are you doing triathlons? Most people's reasons for doing triathlons include a desire to be fit for life, mentally and physically; to test yourself with new challenges and to experience the fun and social rewards of training and competing.

Realistic targets

How much time can you reasonably devote to training? You have to organise your training so that it complements your work and family life, instead of getting in the way of it. It should help you deal with stress in your life, not create it. This should influence the targets you set yourself.

Enjoyable sessions

If you aren't enjoying your training, you won't be able to keep it up. It is crucial that you don't push yourself too hard.

Sportsmen at the top of their game have described the experience of being in "the zone". Boris Becker said that a tennis ball would seem like a football; he couldn't fail. David Beckham is reported to have visualised beforehand the perfectly placed free kick that took England to the World Cup Finals in 2002. They are in a state where their bodies know what to do and they just have to stay out of the way and enjoy the ride. This comes from practising until reactions and movements become internalised i.e. beyond intellectual deliberation.

Ordinary triathletes can also enjoy this state but only if we make the decision to stay within our limits. When we are trying our hardest to swim, cycle or run faster, the chances are that we will lose our co-ordination and poise. When swimming, we will pull harder and harder and forget to glide, when running, we will pull our head down into our body and tighten up, when cycling, we will lose our rhythm and forget to let the bike do the work. Triathletes can enter the zone whenever we decide to throw away our egotistical motivations, go with the flow of movement, and enjoy the present moment.

There was a story in a magazine in the 1980s of an elite runner who practised yoga and completed a full marathon breathing completely through his nose. He reported that as well as producing his best ever time this gave him a sense of ease, relaxation, increased energy and, most importantly of all, enjoyment. The nose is designed by nature for breathing. Breathing through the mouth should really only happen in times of stress.

When we are training and competing in triathlons, we want to be in a natural state, not under stress. But pushing ourselves too hard is interfering with nature. When we tighten up and our breathing becomes laboured, we aren't behaving naturally. To be natural is to be poised. Truly great athletes can be poised while pushing themselves to the limits. Most professional athletes don't quite have that quality but compensate with commitment and guts. It was impressive to watch British runner Roger Black produce the performance of a lifetime for his Olympic 400 metres Silver medal in 1996. He was racing against Michael Johnson. Over the last 100 metres, Black grimaced with determination and pain as Johnson cruised home. Black was delighted with silver, his greatest career achievement, because he accepted that Johnson was 'in a different class'.

Zen in the water

Here are seven ways to be a Zen Triathlete.

1. Plan an achievable number of sessions per week.

A realistic weekly plan could be

Sunday: Long bike ride (2-3 hours), including a stop for a cup of tea half way.

With the right bike, you can't help but go at a taxing pace. The machine helps you ride fast.

Wednesday and Saturday: Run - up to 30 minutes, different routes/ terrains, varying intensity from easy jog to hard run, depending on your mood. Run like an African hunter –head poised on top of your lengthening spine – top of the head to the sky, tail to the floor.

Monday and Friday: Swim - 45 minutes each including rest times - using interval training and always working primarily on technique. Enjoy the flow of your body moving through the water instead of placing emphasis on pulling with muscular effort in your shoulders.

Have a stretching session every day. You can do this while watching television. See point 2.

Having fun preparing.

2. Enjoy stretching

Stretching is good for flexibility, breathing, and a general spring in your step. It will help to prevent injury and improve your awareness of your body.

Allow 20 to 30 minutes for a good stretching session. See it as a chance to unwind and get in touch with your body. Take time over each stretch, which should feel good, not painful. Many triathletes rush through stretches, bouncing up and down and getting them over and done with. This approach to stretching will be of limited benefit.

Speed work and weight training are essential components in a top athlete's training schedule but, if your goals are simply aerobic fitness and enjoyment of triathlons, you are unlikely to need them. Triathlon training should reward you with the health benefits of improved cardiovascular function, muscle tone and weight management. But stretching is a very worthwhile addition to aerobic training.

Recommended reading is Stretching by Bob Anderson. See Further Reading. This guides you clearly through all the stretches you'll need.

3. Work on technique over fitness

Ian Thorpe was described by Simon Barnes, in The Times during the Athens Olympic Games, as languid, serene and Zen-like. Michael Phelps prepared for his races listening to hard rap music on his headphones.

His swimming looked like an expression of anger. People compete for different reasons but it makes more sense from a health point of view to aim to be like Thorpe. Fittingly, in the 200-metre showdown between the two, Thorpe won convincingly.

4. Be realistic about the kind of triathlete you can be

Other triathletes may be doing more training than you but there is no point in comparing yourself to them. To complete even a 'Try a Tri' event is a great accomplishment. To do it without stress or strain would be an even greater one. So long as your attitude is right, this should be achievable for you.

5. Pay more attention to how you feel than what your stopwatch tells you

When people talk about personal bests, they are usually referring to times recorded. But what about the condition you're in at the end of a training session or race? Surely the quality of your experience is more significant than the satisfaction you gain from improved times.

6. Think tall

Founder of The Alexander Technique, FM Alexander, explained that we can't directly *do* anything to attain poise because it is something that is natural but, in most people and in most activities, lost. Instead of *doing* anything to be more poised, we have to *think*. The thoughts that he recommended are:

Let the neck be free so that the head goes forward and up (think forward through the face and up through the crown of your head), and the back lengthens and widens. In other words, poise means that the head is free on top of the spine and the spine is lengthening with the back not hunched or unduly arched, so that natural breathing can occur. It is worth having

some Alexander Technique lessons to get an idea of the meaning of these words and the sense of poise that follows. See **www.stat.org.uk** for a list of teachers.

7. Actively rest your back

Wilfred Barlow in The Alexander Principle (Gollancz 1973) emphasises the importance of being able to return to a "balanced state of rest". This means becoming aware of unwanted tension throughout your head, neck and back and letting it go. Alexander recommended lying down on a hard surface with feet on the floor, knees up and the head gently raised on a few books. (See photo on page 15.)

Think of your neck being free without doing anything to free it. Give the weight of your head to the books. Be aware of the wholeness of your back, including your pelvis. Think the crown of the head away from your spine and allow your back to spread out against the floor, or table, lengthening and widening. Send your shoulders one away from the other. Point your knees up to the ceiling.

Final thought

If you push yourself too hard, aiming for super fitness or dramatically improved race performances, you run the risk of burning yourself out. If every training session feels like hard work and you have to force yourself to go out and do it, something is wrong. You'll either get injured or begin to find other reasons not to train. But if you enjoy training for the sake of training and let it become a kind of Zen, it will be a way of life you'll want to continue. So the most important element of your triathlon training needs to be enjoyment.

(1) This idea is explored in Fitness without Stress, Rickover, 1988, Metamorphous Press and The Art of Swimming, Shaw and D'Angour, 1996, Ashgrove Publishing.

Swimming Injuries
Prevention is Better than Cure

Working on front crawl
technique instead of rushing.

The most important thing for you to monitor in order to prevent injuries is your attitude. The more successful you become at something, the harder it is to change and, in general, the better the athlete, the less humility there is as to the cause of injuries. In other words, the athlete doesn't see he or she may be doing something wrong. For elite athletes, with their high training volume, staying injury free is difficult. But this doesn't mean picking up injuries is inevitable. Most swimming injuries are preventable, caused by a mixture of over training and inappropriate technique and will respond best to you seeking the underlying cause of the problem so you can make changes.

Because the water supports you, taking the pressure from your joints, swimming can be your chance to release and expand. For triathletes, it is an opportunity to undo some of the knots you have created during hard rides or long runs and energise stiff, sore muscles. But for many triathletes, swimming will be just as injurious as running and possibly more so than cycling. This is because, in a quest for the fastest possible times, your inclination may be to fight the water instead of enjoying the experience of moving through it; to push yourself instead of learning how you can swim with less effort, greater efficiency and ultimately more speed. The less proficient a swimmer you are, the harder you are likely to try. But just gritting your teeth and working harder isn't the way forward, particularly if you want to avoid injury.

Here's how to avoid some of the most common problems from swimming front crawl:

Child learning principles of front crawl.

Headaches and neck and back pains

Changing your head position

The first thing to look at is the position of your head. Pulling your head back against your spine will create tension in your neck, which may lead to headaches, and compression of your spine, which may lead to lower back problems. On land, the crown of your head should lead your spine upwards against gravity as you move in a vertical plane. When swimming, for the crown of your head to lead your lengthening spine, you need to release the weight of your head into the water, from the atlanto-occipital joint between your ears, and look at the floor. This fishlike movement of your head and spine should be the foundation of your front crawl. In open-water swimming for triathlons, you will need to lift your head to look where you are going but avoid fixing it in a forward-looking position. While pulling the head back against the spine and hollowing the back is injurious in itself, swimming front crawl from this poor foundation additionally puts strain on your shoulders because a tense back impairs freedom of movement of limbs.

Rotating your body

With your head still, you should roll your body from side to side. Swimming flat, with your hips fixed, impedes shoulder roll and puts strain on the middle of your back as well as the shoulders. Rolling your hips and shoulders in tandem keeps your back in one piece. To inhale, if you don't roll your body, you have to crane your neck, which creates strain from the base of your neck to the middle of your back. Roll your whole body and turn your head. Aim to be in a balanced position with your face out of the water where, with one arm extended, and legs kicking, you could keep moving forward. Avoid interrupting the flow of the stroke, going off balance by pulling your head out of the water and snatching a breath. Only your mouth and nose need to clear the water. Lifting your whole head out of the water puts enormous strain on your neck and back, as well as the opposite shoulder. Keep one ear in the water and continue pointing the crown of your head forward, in the same direction as your spine.

A free neck for the bike and run

In triathlon races, the worst start you can give yourself is a headache and tight back from the swim. It is equally worthwhile to consider the poise of the head on the spine during the land-based triathlon segments. When riding, think of the crown of your head moving away from your spine. Think of the whole of your spine lengthening, right down to the tail. When looking ahead, keep the back of your neck soft and move your head from the joint in between your ears. Avoid shortening your neck and back by fixing your head in a forward-looking position. When running, your head should be free on top of your spine. Looking ahead, let your head lead you forwards (where you want to go) and upwards (against gravity) so that your spine lengthens and you stay light on your feet. For more information on running with the Alexander Technique, see The Art of Running, by Malcolm Balk. See Further Reading.

Shoulder problems

The shoulder is a flexible but unstable part of the anatomy. The vulnerability of the area is the price we pay for the excellent flexibility of the joint. This flexibility enables us to carry out the myriad movements, in all directions, that we make with our hands and arms. When swimming front crawl, you will benefit from viewing the shoulder as the part of your body that enables you to move your hand in a full circle at your side, under and over the water.

Use your hips

Belief that all the power of the front crawl stroke comes from the shoulder, and underestimation of the importance of the hips and torso, may cause shoulder problems. Without overstretching your shoulder, roll on to your side as you extend the forward arm. Think of extending from your hip to your fingers. Let the catch phase, where you get hold of the water ready to pull yourself through it with your hand, be a non- doing movement, with the shoulder staying soft and elbow still, as your palm moves downwards. The pull phase should involve the hip roll as your opposite arm extends forwards.

Work on a gentler arm recovery

A high elbow is an important feature of the front crawl. It facilitates a good "pull", hip roll and a clean entry of the hand into the water. But many swimmers, encouraged by drills such as "chicken wings" and "zipper arm", put huge strain on the shoulder by lifting the elbow out of the water. Standing on dry land, if you put your hand on your shoulder and lift the elbow towards the ceiling, you can feel the tension in your shoulder. Imagine doing this a few hundred times in succession and it is easy to see how swimming front crawl can be hazardous. To avoid this, let your hand scull underwater all the way to your hip, turning to allow your thumb to leave the water first. Point your hand to the ceiling and then leave your elbow high as you release your hand towards the water. Your arm makes a natural arc and your shoulders will be happier with this movement.

Child learning to relax neck on back.

Enter wider

Another way swimmers strain their shoulders is by entering the hands too close to, or even across, the centre-line of the body. Standing on dry land, feel your shoulder as you put your hand out in front of you. Notice the difference when your hand is directly in front of your shoulder instead of your head. When swimming front crawl, you should constantly work to keep your back wide and shoulders free, one away from the other. Keep space in your armpits. While you should be rolling from one side to the other, it is important to remember to keep your left arm to the left of your head and spine and your right arm right. Think of swimming along two railway tracks instead of a monorail.

Cramp

Soften your ankles

For front crawl kick, you need to loosen your ankles so your feet act like flippers as they move from the "hinge". If you soften the front of your ankle, do nothing with the feet and kick from the hips, you will experience the flipper effect. But if you try to *do* a flipper like movement by pointing your toes and actively moving your feet, your calf muscles become overly contracted and there is a high chance you will suffer cramp. To treat cramp, rub the area vigorously to warm and increase blood supply to it.

Final thought

If you need help in changing your attitude, a contrast in the styles of Olympic swimmers Ian Thorpe and Michael Phelps was pointed out by Simon Barnes in The Times on August 16th 2004.

"There is a sweet yin and yang contrast… Thorpe swims in a sort of passionless perfection, his style looks nothing less than languid… Thorpe has serenity about him: Phelps has anything but. There is a touch of Zen in the way Thorpe moves through the water: Lord knows what religious comparison you can make with Phelps. Something involving human sacrifice, perhaps."

If you decide to make the water your friend and learn to enjoy the help it gives you in letting go and moving freely, your stroke will improve and you will be less prone to injury.

Letting go in breast stroke.

Eight Week Training Plan

Here is a possible eight-week training plan for a novice triathlete preparing for a short course event with a 500-metre swim. Swimming sessions enable you to keep your training going when your legs are tired or sore after the previous day's long ride or run.

This is just to give you an idea of how swim training could fit into an overall triathlon-training plan. I have included a rest day in every week.

Interval Training

Interval training involves splitting your total training distance into a chosen number of smaller distances, aiming to complete these distances in a target time, and including a period of rest in between each distance. Combined with your cycle and running training, you should aim to do two to three sessions per week.

Warm up/ swimming technique work

Every session should include a warm up consisting of these elements. I would recommend a warm up like this for all levels. Novices may do less, advanced swimmers more. Cool downs should also include these elements.

Gliding

● Always start with some gliding, working on freeing your neck, breathing gently and letting your back lengthen and widen.
  25 - 50 metres (see Lesson 1).

Working on back

● Swim 50 - 100 metres on your back. Work on letting the water support your head and upper back, widening across your shoulders, sending your sacrum and coccyx away from your head.
  50 – 100 metres (see Lesson 2).

Front crawl 150– 250 metres

● Do some work on side balance in front crawl: 6 kicks with one arm extended and face in and stop. Repeat with other arm extended.

● Swim front crawl, kicking six times on each side to exaggerate the glide idea.

● Practise the breathing position, kicking on your side, releasing your head into the water but with your face out (one ear in the water and top of your head pointing forwards). Work on finding this position from swimming with your face in the water. Also work on returning your face to the water from the breathing position. (See Lessons 4 and 5)

Always do some work on side balance with face out of water.

WEEK 1	
Sunday	**Long bike ride**
Monday	**SWIM (1200M)** **Warm up** (400m) *See warm up / technique instructions on page 54.* **Set (500m)** 10 x 50 m on 1:30 *See if you can keep your pace. E.g 10 x 1 minute swims.* **Rest** 2 minutes. **Cool down/ technique** 300m *Choose elements from warm up. Include some easy work on back.*
Tuesday	Run
Wednesday	Bike
Thursday	**SWIM (1200M)** **Warm up/ technique** (400m) **Set (500m)** 5 x 100 on 2.30 6/10 perceived effort ratio. *Aim for consistency, e.g 5 x 2 minute swims* *Take your time when turning to inhale.* **Rest** 2 minutes **Cool down** 300m
Friday	**Run**
Saturday	**REST**

WEEK 2	
Sunday	**Long Run**
Monday	**SWIM (1300M)** **Warm up/ technique** (400m) **Set (600m)** 3 x 200 m on 6 minutes *Aim for three identical times and identical stroke counts (strokes taken per length).* **Rest** 2 minutes. **Cool down** 300m
Tuesday	**Bike**
Wednesday	**REST**
Thursday	**Run**
Friday	**SWIM (1300M)** **Warm up/ technique** (400m) **Set (600m)** 2x 300m on 8 minutes *Medium to fast pace 80% perceived effort rate.* *Aim for consistency. E.g 2 x 6 minute swims, without feeling exhausted at the end.* **Rest** 2 minutes. **Cool down** 300m
Saturday	**Run**

WEEK 3	
Sunday	**Bike**
Monday	**Run**
Tuesday	**SWIM (1200M)**
	Warm up/ technique (400m)
	Set (500m)
	500 metre time trial.
	Aim for even 100 metre splits.
	Keep your stroke long, rolling the hips and gliding with the forward arm extended. Take your time on the in-breath.
	Aim for the 100 metre split times achieved in your 300 metre swims last week.
	Rest 2 minutes.
	Cool down 300m
Wednesday	**Bike**
Thursday	**REST**
Friday	**Run**
Saturday	**SWIM (1450M)**
	Warm up/ technique (400m)
	Set (750m)
	10 x 75 m on 2 mins
	Aim for consistency throughout first 7 and see if you can make last 3 x75s increasingly faster.
	Rest 2 minutes.
	Cool down 300m

WEEK 4	
Sunday	Bike
Monday	REST
Tuesday	Run
Wednesday	**SWIM 1500M** **Warm up/ Technique** (400m) **Set (800m)** 2x 400metre 1 minute's rest in between swims. *First 400 easy, second repeat faster than first.* **Rest** 2 minutes. **Cool down** 300m
Thursday	**Bike**
Friday	**SWIM 1500M** **Warm up/ technique** (400m) **Set (800m)** Easy up faster down 50m easy pace 100m 150m 200m medium pace 150m 100m 50 m fast pace 10 – 20 seconds rest between swims. **Rest** 2 minutes. **Cool down** 300m
Saturday	**Run**

WEEK 5	
Sunday	**Long bike ride**
Monday	**SWIM (1500M)** **Warm up** (400m) **Set (800m)** 8 x 75 m on 2 mins (600m) *See if you can keep a consistent pace.* 1 min rest 4 x 50 on 1.20 (200m) **Rest** 2 minutes. **Cool down/ technique** 300m *Choose elements from warm up. Include some easy work on back.*
Tuesday	**Run**
Wednesday	**REST**
Thursday	**SWIM (1500M)** **Warm up/ technique** (400m) **Set (800m)** 8 x 100 on 2.15 *70 % perceived effort ratio.* *Aim for consistency, e.g 8 x 1:55 min .swims.* *Take your time when turning to inhale.* **Rest** 2 minutes. **Cool down** 300m
Friday	**Run**
Saturday	**Bike**

WEEK 6	
Sunday	**Long Run**
Monday	**SWIM (1500M)** **Warm up/ technique** (400 m) **Set (800m)** 3x 200m on 5 minutes (600m) *Aim for three identical times and identical stroke counts* *(strokes taken per length).* 2 x 100 on 2.10 increase pace from 200s. **Rest** 2 minutes. **Cool down** 300 m
Tuesday	**Bike**
Wednesday	**REST**
Thursday	**Run**
Friday	**SWIM (1600M)** **Warm up/ technique** (400m) **Set (900m)** 3x 300m on 7.30 mins *Medium 70 to 80 per cent perceived effort rate.* *Aim for consistency.* *E.g 3 x 6 minute swims, without feeling exhausted at the end.* **Rest** 2 minutes. **Cool down** 300m
Saturday	**Run**

WEEK 7	
Sunday	**Bike**
Monday	**Run**
Tuesday	**SWIM 1500M** **Warm up/ technique** (400m) **Set 1 (500m)** 500 metre time trial. *Aim for even 100 metre splits.* *Keep your stroke long, rolling the hips and gliding with the forward arm extended. Take your time on the in-breath.* *Compare time with week 3.* **Rest** 1 minute. **Set 2 (200m)** 8 x 25m on 15secs race pace (should feel easy). **Rest** 2 minutes. **Cool down** 300m
Wednesday	**Bike**
Thursday	**REST**
Friday	**Run**
Saturday	**SWIM (1450M)** **Warm up/ technique** (400m) **Set (750m)** 10 x 75 m on 2 mins *70 per cent effort rate.* *Aim for consistency throughout.* *Compare times with week 3.* **Rest** 2 minutes. **Cool down** 300m

WEEK 8	
Sunday	Bike
Monday	REST
Tuesday	Run
Wednesday	**SWIM 1600M** **Warm up/ Technique** (400m) **Set (900m)** 6 x 150 metres 30 secs rest between swims. *First 2 repeats 60 % effort, second 2 , 80%, last 2, 70%* **Rest** 2 minutes. **Cool down** 300m
Thursday	**Bike**
Friday	**SWIM 1500M** **Warm up/ technique** (400m) **Set (800m)** Easy up faster down 50m easy pace 100m 150m 200m medium pace 150m 100m 50 m fast pace 10 – 20 seconds rest between swims. *Compare times with week 3.* **Rest** 2 minutes. **Cool down** 300m
Saturday	**Run**

Swimming Holidays

Could a Swimming Holiday help you?

- *Are you one of thousands of non-swimmers in Britain whose needs - to overcome fear of water and learn to move freely enough to exercise without strain - have not been met by conventional instruction?*

  We will lead you step by step through the transition from non-swimmer to swimmer, helping you to become at home in the water through individual attention and hands on guidance and support.

- *Do you swim for health benefits but suspect you may be doing yourself more harm than good? This may be the case if you swim with the head held out of the water, struggle with breathing or get any aches and pains after swimming.*

  We will show you how to swim more smoothly and efficiently by learning to prevent unnecessary tension.

- *Do you put a lot of effort into swimming but feel you aren't really getting anywhere?*

  We will help you to eliminate instinctive movement patterns, especially when moving the head to inhale, which hinder your progress through water.

- *Do you enjoy swimming but feel you could get more out of it with a better understanding of how the strokes work?*

  We will teach you the importance of allowing the water to support you and gliding in all the strokes instead of putting all the emphasis on propulsive movements.

- *Are you a triathlete whose weakest discipline is swimming or a budding triathlete lacking the confidence to compete in a swimming race?*

  We will show you how to enjoy swimming longer distances without straining or exhausting yourself so you can get out of the water fresh for a bike ride!

"Thank you for your patience with me during my lessons. Goodness knows how you even persuaded me to get into the pool, let alone glide!...I now have no fear at all and am attempting breast stroke.... This has been a very hard thing for me to conquer and your approach was enormously helpful and positive."
Lesley, Kent

"Many thanks for all your help and patience throughout the week. It's been a great experience – can now try all those watersports!" Justin, Southampton

Benefits of a Swimming Holiday in Cardigan Bay

- Individual attention enables you to go at your own pace. Groups are inevitably made up of people with different abilities, which may be intimidating or frustrating.

- Hands on guidance and support, with the instructor in the water. This promotes release of unnecessary tension and encourages you to find the support of the water. It also helps you learn new movement patterns.

- The Alexander Technique helps you to become aware of and give up unnecessary tension. It is useful for all levels of swimmer to improve your relationship with the water. You learn the importance of the head/ neck/ back relationship and the link between this and breathing.

Usually when people learn to swim, their fear of water leads to unnecessary tension in every new movement they learn. This pattern of tension then becomes part of the movement - a habit - and begins to feel normal. Our approach helps you prevent unnecessary tension so you can learn or relearn to swim freely.

- With intensive, individual lessons, you can make a lot of progress in a short space of time. When learning through weekly lessons, momentum can be lost.

- Quiet, warm, same-depth pool, with sauna and steam-room. There is the opportunity for all pupils to practise between lessons in the same pool.

- Courses tailor made to suit you. As well as the standard weekly course of eight 40-minute lessons, we offer weekend breaks, long weekend breaks and midweek breaks. Also shared lessons for couples. There is also flexibility regarding length of lesson.

- Beautiful coastal location. Cardigan is the gateway to the stunning Pembrokeshire National Park, with 180 miles of coastal path and the even less explored Preseli mountains, and Cardigan Bay, with its high population of bottlenose dolphins, easily spotted from lovely Mwnt beach, 2 minutes' drive from the pool.

"Instruction excellent. Very hands on which is needed, very flexible – moves at your pace rather than imposing a standard timetable…. I was very pleased indeed with my progress. The whole experience is very good. What a shame a) that all teaching for adults isn't like this and b) that I didn't find you sooner!"
Ian, Surrey

"I really am so pleased that I have been able to change my relationship with water through your warm and thoughtful approach to helping and teaching me last week." *Jennie, London*

Our Approach to Teaching Children

Five year old learner

With a five-year old child our aim in a course of 6 x 30 minute- lessons is for him/ her to be

 happy and independent in the water

 able to swim with the face in and get the head out to breathe

able to swim on the back without strain by allowing the water to support the head.

Using the principles of the Alexander Technique, we use a hands-on teaching method and remain in the water throughout the lesson.

The emphasis from the first lesson is on making friends with the water by learning to breathe naturally into it and experience the buoyancy of the head.

If the child isn't ready to swim independently, this doesn't mean the lessons won't be successful in establishing his/ her enjoyment of being in the water.

Sometimes it is appropriate for parents to get in the water so that we can show you how to work with your child, without using buoyancy aids, to continue the work when you go home.

"Robyn (5) wanted you to know that she managed to jump in without holding onto someone and also swam under water well today . She is now an expert and likes to tell everyone else where they are going wrong. We both very much appreciated your calm teaching even when faced with cries of ' 'NO, NO!' on day one...............
I felt quite emotional when I saw how she managed to float and swim so elegantly on her back so soon" Dr Findlay, Sussex

Seven years upwards

Children of 7 and above are usually ready to learn correct technique.

They tend to be excited by being in water, especially by playing underwater. But when it comes to moving from

A to B, their movements are often frantic and instinctive, producing strain. Their breathing may be erratic, with lots of gasping and holding the breath.

Our aim is to harness their enthusiasm for swimming and channel their energy into moving through water more smoothly by letting go of unnecessary tension. We teach them to glide and breathe freely in all the strokes. They are often surprised that half as many strokes will get them to the end of the pool more quickly.

Our approach is the same for competitive swimmers:

"Laura feels completely brilliant now, like she's been given some special swimming 'secret recipe' that no-one else has!"
Mrs Lacey, Oxfordshire